Are You My MAMA?

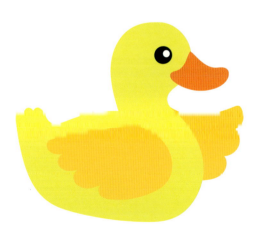

W. Books

"Are you my mama?" asked the little yellow duck.

"No, I am not your mama. I am a Mallard Duck and this is my duckling daughter."

"You are welcome to stay with us, but I am sure there is someone missing you."

"Are you my mama?" asked the little yellow duck.

"No, I am not your mama. I am a Penguin and I live where it is mostly snowy and very cold."

"You are welcome to stay with me, but I think you would like to be somewhere warmer."

"Are you my mama?" asked the little yellow duck.

"No, I am not your mama. I am a Swan, this is my little cygnet son."

"You are welcome to stay with us, but I am sure there is someone missing you."

"You are welcome to stay with me, I stand on one leg much of the time."

"You are welcome to stay with us, but I am sure there is someone missing you."

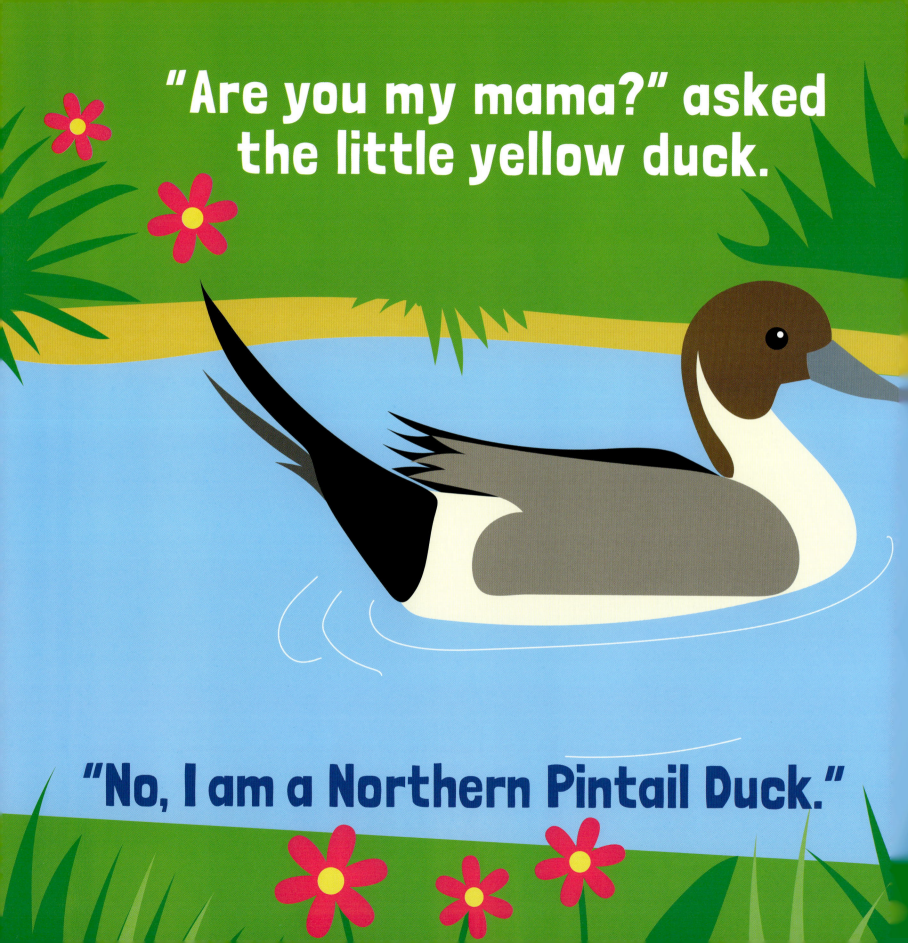

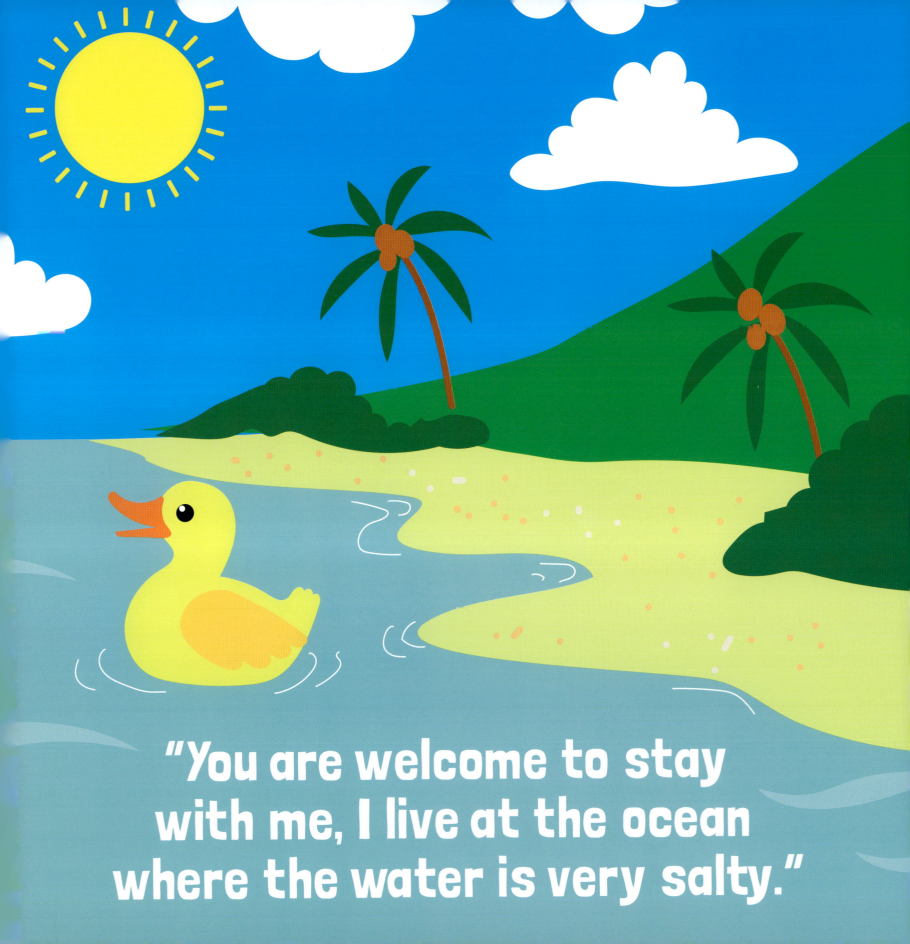

"You are welcome to stay with me, I live at the ocean where the water is very salty."

"You are welcome to stay with us, but I am sure there is someone missing you."

"Are you my mama?" asked the little yellow duck.

"No, I am a Eurasian Teal Duck. These are my many ducklings."

"MY MAMA FOUND ME!" said the very happy little yellow duck.

"And just in time."

"Maddie, it is time for your bath," Maddie's mama calls out.

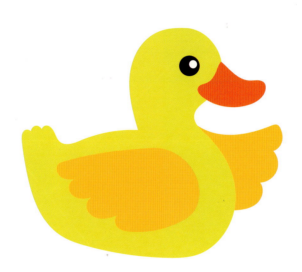